THEY SAY I TALK FUNNY

K.A. Simpson

Copyright 2019. All Rights Reserved.

Published by SparkLight Creative Group, Covington, Kentucky.

No part of this publication may be reproduced, stored in a retrieval system, or transmitted in any form by any means, electronic, mechanical, photocopying, recorded, scanning, or otherwise, except as permitted under Section 107 or 108 of the 1979 United States Copyright Act, without the prior written permission of the publisher.

Printed in the United States of America.

dedicated to…

my grandmother, my mother, and my three younger brothers.

CONTENTS

Entrepreneurship Ain't Just A City in China, 5

A Valley of Entrepreneurial Drama, 12

The Real Education From Lauryn Hill, 20

I'm An Addict, 29

Live Small But Dream Big. 38

Time to Shit or Get Off The Pot, 47

Entrepreneurship Ain't Just A City In China

"If we tried to think of a good idea, we wouldn't have been able to think of a good idea. You just have to find the solution for a problem in your own life." -Brian Chesky, Co-founder of Airbnb

Back in the summer of 1978, as the first child born by way of in vitro fertilization was being ushered into the world, a single mother in Newport, Kentucky was going into labor with her first child. That child would go on to live a life full of ups and downs, taking him to graduate high school at the age of sixteen, to serve in the United States military as a non-commissioned officer and eventually to fulfill his life's dream of becoming an entrepreneur.

In my journey, I've found what works best is to work within a diverse entrepreneurial ecosystem. To build such an ecosystem, leaders across sectors must proactively connect businesses, especially those owned by people of color, along with experts, networks, and resources in a seamless way.

The lack of diversity in business ownership further stifles diversity in entrepreneurship and threatens the long-term economic health of our economy.

Some have attempted to combat this by creating new fund structures to replicate friends and family investments for lower-income and lower-wealth entrepreneurs. We know that a great majority of entrepreneurs draw on their savings to get off the ground, and one in five lean on funds from friends and family members. Having enough capital at the onset is highly correlated with a business' chance of survival. But the enormous racial wealth gap, coupled with the almost complete unavailability of venture capital and loan funding, means that capital is harder to come by for entrepreneurs of color.

In my twenties it would have never crossed my mind that I'd be calling myself an entrepreneur because of a lack of the aforementioned resources. But the more I reflect on the journey that got me here today—specifically the endless nights of trying to discover the next great idea, staying sequestered in my apartment for days at a time, I realize that I was more entrepreneurial than I thought.

Fast forward to the present, a silver lining may have come in one of the most unexpected of places in the Trump Administration's tax overhaul. A little-known provision in the final version signed into law enables states to establish opportunity zones that encourage investors to defer capital gains, so long as they invest in existing or new businesses.

This begins to establish formal mechanisms that connects prominent entrepreneurs with emerging entrepreneurs of color. We know, based on research like Gallup's Builder Profile, that the qualities that characterize successful entrepreneurs don't discriminate by race. But social networks shape perceptions of who can become a successful entrepreneur in the first place. Exposure to business owners in one's own network is a powerful lever. It has been shown to boost the likelihood that someone will become an entrepreneur themselves.

THE FAMILY CELEBRATING MY MOTHER'S GRADUATION FROM NURSING SCHOOL CIRCA 1984 WITH ME IN THE MIDDLE FINISHING OFF SOME OF THE REFRESHMENTS.

Cities like Cincinnati, Ohio are intentionally working to solve that problem. With initial funding from the New York City-based Surdna Foundation, the Cincinnati USA Regional Chamber's Minority Business Accelerator created a resource designed to help entrepreneurs of color connect the dots; focusing on reducing disparity in the region's business community by driving economic activity for African American and Hispanic-owned companies while increasing employment in under-employed segments of the region.

With that being said, for me, the last two decades seem to have flown by. I've come to the realization that there are moments throughout life when time seems compressed, when so many shocking and life changing events crowd together. Do you remember the day when Netscape, one of the first internet browsers, became a $2 billion company? What about when Amazon upended our online expectations by introducing 1-Click shopping? How about when Napster, another throwback of music downloading platforms, faced down Metallica or when Twitter showed us what was really happening on the streets of Tehran? These are the moments of innovation that changed how we interacted with the rest of the world.

This new economic superpower has the potential of being even more effective if the fastest growing segments of our population—people of color—continue to be able to start businesses at an increasing rate.

Or should we look to new types of entrepreneurship? Like a style of entrepreneurship that solves problems while making a profit.

A start-up, backed by rapper T.I., launched a free mobile service for low-income communities called Moolah Mobile. This service turns Android devices into advertising platforms. According to a press release, the service will provide free talk, text, and data to an estimated 1 million users in select U.S. states over the duration of the partnership by subsidizing their wireless bills with income generated by Moolah Mobile on their smartphones. In the Greater Cincinnati area, the owners of Carabello Coffee geared their business model toward philanthropy with a plan to use their profits to directly benefit works of compassion in coffee-producing countries. In 2001, I worked at my local library where I taught a series of computer classes, one of which was how to create a resume. Now, back then, the general public was not as agile navigating Microsoft Word and Google docs wasn't even thought of yet. So I realized there was a demand for someone to just stylize a resume—after several of my students asked me to take a crack at their resumes for them. So, in 2004, I began the process of making a business out of this service. That was my first business. And it was the first time that I envisioned an avenue for us non-traditional entrepreneurs to harness the long-dormant power of lower-income and lower-wealth Americans while helping them to move ahead in life.

I'll be the first to say that it ain't easy. I've worked with startups, designed business plans, and even added services to my own ventures. None of this happened overnight, but more importantly, I didn't do any of it with the intention of simply becoming a millionaire...nor did I do it alone.

A Valley of Entrepreneurial Drama

"Nothing's more dangerously powerful than an intelligent creative." - K.A. Simpson

An ecosystem oozing with entrepreneurial spirit can spur advancements in unlikely places...like my hometown of Cincinnati, Ohio. Okay, for the sake of not being called out by those who I grew up with, my hometown is actually the smaller town of Covington, Kentucky, the city just south of Cincinnati.

Cincinnati and Covington don't just share opposing banks of the Ohio River. Both of their downtown regions reside in the same valley surrounded by hills. A valley which lends to the area's unlikely settlement in the 1700's and, in some way, explains its recent resurgence as an entrepreneurial mecca.

Struggling from the exhausting effort of re-emerging from the shadow of being called a fly-over city for decades, the Greater Cincinnati area has added entrepreneurship to its list of niche industries to create a makers culture that's changing the face of business not seen since the Industrial Revolution.

Cincinnati has long embraced entrepreneurs. They include William Procter, James Gamble, Carl Lindner, and generations of farmers and butchers who populated our Findlay Market, just to name a few. Recently, the area has built on that history with start-up incubators like MORTAR and The Brandery in addition to business development opportunities like SpringBoard Cincinnati.

This has led to a growing number of entrepreneurs to see the Greater Cincinnati area as a welcoming and supportive place for innovation. The area's unconventional urban renewal, especially in Cincinnati's Over-the-Rhine neighborhood and Covington's Downtown area, have become a magnet for entrepreneurs to settle. Yet another draw is the low cost of living, generally low unemployment, and access to major higher education institutions.

But is this entrepreneurial mecca ripe for all entrepreneurs?

It's been said (and proven in many cases) that people of color have to work twice as hard to get half as much as our white counterparts. Many of us know we pay a high "Black Tax" assessed through biased hiring practices, pay disparity, unequal promotion, unfair housing and urban renewal projects. People of color constantly fight for equality as well as equity.

The summer of 2016 saw traditional media outlets outsmarted by social media that served as first notice to the murders of Alton Sterling and Philando Castile who were two Black men shot and killed by police officers. It was on July 5th of that year when the former of the two was shot several times at close range while held down on the ground by two Baton Rouge, Louisiana police officers. The next day, the latter of the two men was fatally shot by a police officer in Falcon Heights, Minnesota. The posts on social media documented, in real time, how a chance encounter with a police officer could end a life.

TEACHING *PUB_INC*, A BOOK PUBLISHING INCUBATOR, AT THE ART ACADEMY OF CINCINNATI.

Would this have happened if these two men were not Black? The question is an echo of that asked by Minnesota Governor Mark Dayton at a news conference the day following Castile's murder. Spurring from those events, what began as a peaceful protest in Dallas, ended with a lone sniper wounding seven innocent protesters and killing five police officers.

To it's still hard to imagine how these three occurrences could happen in a country that has come so far. Did we not learn our lesson with Rodney King? King was beaten by Los Angeles Police officers following a high-speed car chase on March 3, 1991. Despite the incident being filmed, three of the four officers involved were acquitted of all charges, serving as a catalyst for the 1992 Los Angeles Riots, where 55 people were killed and over 2,000 were injured.

The shooting of black men at the hands of police officers seem to be a part of some gruesome loop of events. For the Black community, the threat of police abuse has simply become a part of life; a life lesson reserved for Black males only.

Cincinnati too is not immune.

Think back to Cincinnati's very own civil unrest which snapped up the nation's attention in 2001. This was the year when the 15th young Black male, since 1995, was gunned down by Cincinnati police officers. Quickly after the civil unrest subsided, the Cincinnati Police Department (CPD), prompted by a lawsuit by the American Civil Liberties Union (ACLU), adopted a collaborative agreement which spelled out how CPD should follow a community focused approach towards policing with the end goal of dramatically changing policies and how new recruits are trained.

Fast forward to 2015 where University of Cincinnati Police Officer Ray Tensing fatally shot Sam DuBose, a Black motorist, during an off-campus traffic stop because of a missing license plate. The campus officer claimed he was forced to fire his weapon after almost being run over by DuBose's car but due to body camera footage contradicting the officer's report, Tensing was indicted on murder and voluntary manslaughter charges which resulted in a hung jury.

Despite the previous, Greater Cincinnati and Northern Kentucky have become a hotbed for innovation and the area now supports an extensive, thriving small business culture. The area also hosts a great number of charitable organizations. Many organizations have made it their goal to leverage these attributes by creating a space where they can help small business owners and entrepreneurs while supporting great causes.

One long-established player in the field of local entrepreneurship is Norwood, Ohio's Hamilton County Business Center (HCBC), which has been home to more than 260 business startups since 1989. Another example is The Center for Great Neighborhoods in Covington, Kentucky, one of the most recent organizations to step up to provide entrepreneurs a platform to succeed and reclaim a long and proud tradition of small business growth. Tom DiBello, longtime executive director, is a transplant to the area from Philadelphia. Perhaps nothing personifies how much entrepreneurship merges with a makers culture as much as the work being done by the organization than with the opening of the Hellmann Creative Center, where the organization is headquartered, along with the nine artist studios the building houses. The Center epitomizes the spirit of creatives in both their entrepreneurial spirit and their creative drive.

In addition, what the Greater Cincinnati area does well is develop strong government initiatives which give innovators the kind of information they need for problem solving, which can result in an exciting new improved quality of life. The City of Cincinnati has especially capitalized on the start-up energy by creating its own minority business initiative and partnering with like-minded organizations like MORTAR. MORTAR aims to lend a voice to traditionally marginalized entrepreneurs. Being an organization founded by three millennial-aged Black men helps MORTAR to uniquely position itself as a link to those they serve. Some of the organization's present initiatives include its Entrepreneurship Academy, providing space at pop-up shops in Cincinnati's traditionally marginalized neighborhoods of Over-the-Rhine and Walnut Hills, and offering low-interest start-up capital through their Iron Chest Fund.

Diversity and inclusion strategies are being undertaken and implemented by many corporations as well. If you are running your own business, big corporations looking for diverse suppliers are on the rise. Hopefully, we will begin to see the "Black Tax" dissipate.

The Real Education From Lauryn Hill

"Music has healing power. It has the ability to take people out of themselves for a few hours." - Elton John

Successful startup founders are often hailed as superhuman, but the reality is they're regular people like you and me. Well, maybe not exactly.

Given the unusual lifestyle of an entrepreneur, and that so many are fueled by the promise of wild riches, it comes as no surprise that many startup founders share inspirational stories about overcoming adversity. And many quote some sort of inspirational item that helped get them through those hard times.

My inspiration has always been music.

We all have a soundtrack to our lives. Some are an eclectic mashup of county and rock and roll. Some soundtracks simply stay within one genre. My soundtrack comprises a little of all the above. But there are three artists' work which has stayed on high rotation throughout my entire life. For the first 20 years of my life it was a toss-up between Whitney Houston, Michael Jackson and Aretha Franklin. But when I turned 20, an album was released that dropped into my soul and expanded my mind.

MEETING A POP CULTURE ICON, JOHN WATERS, WITH FRIENDS.

On August 25, 1998, Ms. Lauryn Hill released her solo debut album, *The Miseducation of Lauryn Hill* and immediately became a standard in my internal soundtrack. It arrived into my world at a time that my life was in a phase of transition. I was living away from home to the first time in my life an in much need of grounding. This album also came at a time when hip-hop was emerging as a commercial powerhouse, just a year-and-a-half after hip-hop lost the second of its legendary rap giants, when the Notorious B.I.G. was murdered on March 9, 1997 following the death of Tupac Shakur on September 13, 1996. Ms. Hill stuck her foot in it for delivering a cyclone of an album whose tremendous depth resonated throughout my soul and is still being felt today.

At the time of release, hip-hop was struggling to find its own identity—nestled uncomfortably between the identities of R&B and Rap. What helped to make this particular album stand out was that it could school both genres.

A far cry from today's rap, where there is more singing than rapping, the art of rap in the late 1990's still hung close to its origins emitting intermittent and indiscriminate violence making it hard for America to legitimize its existence. With *Miseducation*, Hill was jutted into America's living rooms. This happened, of course, also due to her starring role alongside Whoopi Goldberg in *Sister Act 2: Back in the Habit* and her popularity as being a member of another one of the groups on my internal soundtrack, The Fugees, Hill was, in some circles, being called an unconventional pop princess.

However, when Hill swept the Grammy's Pop category in 1999, she shifted the definition of pop music and made sure no one would ever consider her to be "other" again.

It's an understatement that in 2019, just over twenty years since its release, *The Miseducation of Lauryn Hill* has earned its protected platinum status of most every musical genre. Just like a fine Kentucky bourbon, her melodic syncopations have aged incredibly well to shift our society's consciousness without us even knowing. Hill's reactionary solo album definitely schooled the Grammy Awards' perception of hip-hop that year, at a time when the award show was working on the tail end of about a decade of ignoring the fact that rap was a viable art form.

Throughout the early years of rap in the 1980's, it struggled to be adequately and respectfully recognized by the Recording Academy. On February 24, 1999, Hill made history at the 41st Grammy Awards when she was the first hip-hop artist to win the Grammy for Album of the Year. She also was the first woman to take home five Grammy Awards in one night. Those were two milestones for music genres, thanks to Lauryn Hill... one for hip-hop and one for women in music.

Singing and rapping were always play-cousins yet identifying both as hip-hop was something many struggled with. Perhaps it was the street hustler image of rap in the '80s and '90s mixed with the super-smooth romanticism of R&B in the '90s New Jack Swing Era that made it so difficult to believe the two could fit together under one umbrella. Hill did that. She planted the seed with "Killing Me Softly" on The Fugees' *The Score* album two years prior, but *Miseducation* made it ever more apparent of her pop royalty status.

It was Hill who poured her feelings into a hip-hop album. *Miseducation* tackled love lost, distrust, pregnancy, and self-actualization. At 23 years old, Hill was trying to figure it all out—and exactly what I was going through at the time of its release. Hill proved that one great idea can change the world. In her case, her great idea was manifested through her debut solo album.

Well here it is… an insight into my internal soundtrack. If you're feeling uninspired and are sick of staring at that same blank canvas you call a workspace, take a listen to these other albums that have inspired me over the years. Call it a playlist that sparked my creativity and helped me to look at my work in a new light.

USHER – *My Way*

In my years just returning home from military service in 2001, I attended the University of Cincinnati. One weekend, I found myself trying to write my 12,000-word dissertation with less time left than I'd hoped. My mind blanked every time I sat down in front of the computer screen to type and I became so infuriated with myself that the only artist I could listen to was USHER whose melodic swoons and vocal runs pulled words out of my quickly disintegrating brain and coaxed them onto the computer screen.

Aretha Franklin – *30 Greatest Hits*

This compilation is one of the most recognizable compilations of hits ever made. For example, on the fourth track, "Dr. Feelgood", Franklin's lilting voice bounces off a lounge-y piano riff accompanied by a complete horn section and an organ, seasoning the song with her Baptist church background. It's enough to get your mind and heartbeat racing, let alone what becomes of your creative prowess once you've listened to all thirty songs.

Jay-Z – *Blueprint*

If you are feeling uninspired, prepare for a mind-alteration when you listen to Jay-Z's twisted but poignant album. The song "Renegade" on its own is a warped rap battle between Jay-Z and Eminem. It's series of melodic down-beated infractions of sound and multitrack voice overlays adds a creative depth that inspired me to want more out of whatever project I was working on at the time. The album will quickly get your mind set on the task at hand. At one point, my task was to come up with a storyline which incorporated a circus of flying gorillas, choreographed dance moves and enough profanity to render it strictly watershed material. Listening to this album helped me through it!

Stevie Wonder – *Innervisions*

Producer, composer, pianist, visionary, and maestro. Wonder reinvents music for the post-Civil Rights era. As a result, *Innervisions* is like a snapshot of Black America, seen through the mind's eye of many of those who have shaped my own life. "Too High" looks at drug addiction. "Living for the City" addresses urban issues, and "Jesus Children of America" conveys the cynicism of some organized religions. But it's his syncopated rhythms and instrumental overhauls which is coupled with the familiarity in the subject matter of his words which makes it a go-to when my creativity is stifled.

AMERICAN EDUCATOR AND MULTI-DISCIPLINE PERFORMANCE ARTIST, TIM'M WEST, READING MY 1ST NON-FICTION SELF PUBLISHED WORK, *GAME ON*.

An Honorable Mention: *The Original Kings of Comedy*

This film/soundtrack isn't anything beyond a large gathering of people having a great time. This is not to say the movie doesn't pack quite a bit of attitude. In fact, it even sparks an occasional thought with its razor-edged observational humor, which surveys Black culture (and society in general) with an always frank, sometimes shocking, but always refreshing attitude.

Many times, I remember having this movie playing in the background when I lived in a fraternity house in college and several of my white fraternity brothers occasionally found themselves confounded by cultural references which simply didn't resonate across racial lines. But, as a whole, when Steve Harvey, D.L. Hughley, Cedric The Entertainer and the late Bernie Mac, addressed a human condition which could be understood by people of many races and touched on issues as universal as hating other people's misbehavin' kids, playing hard-to-reach when bill collectors called on the phone, husbands and wives being misaligned about their sexual expectations and what an adult thinks about a young kid who seems gay. Every time I listen to these four hilarious storytellers, it reminds me of Thanksgiving dinner at my Great-Aunt Sarah's house when I was younger; my mother, my grandmother, her brother, a slew of my uncles and cousins telling stories and laughing at life.

I'm An Addict

"If I can't write...I'm crippled. If I can't create...I'm dead." - K.A. Simpson

There have been many times in my career when I've been labeled compulsive and a work addict. Sometimes the adjectives went as far as me being attached with the moniker of obsessive. Once, one of my employers gave me a written reprimand, saying that I was out of balance and impossible to work with.

Being addicted to your business or never being satisfied with your product is not a bad thing. You just need to transform your single-minded dedication into meaningful work that demonstrates your commitment to success.

Being an addict to entrepreneurship is a subject so interesting that even researchers at the top-ranked business school, Whitman School of Management at Syracuse University in New York, were tempted to do a study on it. In their paper titled, "Habitual Entrepreneurs: Possible Cases of Behavioral Addiction?", they mentioned that habitual entrepreneurs, those who launch multiple startups throughout their careers, display symptoms of behavioral addiction similar to other better-known behavioral addictions, such as gambling or Internet usage.

After reading this, I realized that I definitely had a problem, but it was not with me, but with people who want to stay uncomfortably average. What is killing our society here in America is the disorder of being obsessively and compulsively average. It's us entrepreneurs who are simply in love with the idea of being an entrepreneur and don't just want to be average or ordinary. Our previous success or failure does not necessarily mar our determination to give birth to multiple businesses. We can also substitute addiction for the drive which is commonly visible in all entrepreneurs. Whether the motive is money, fame, or social service, we are all passionately driven by some outside force. We strongly believe in what we do and never flinch from our determination to make things work.

AT CINCINNATI'S BOOKS BY THE BANKS REGIONAL BOOK FESTIVAL PRESENTING MY 1ST SELF-PUBLISHED COLLECTION OF FICTIONAL SHORT STORIES, *CHRONICLES OF A BOY MISUNDERSTOOD*.

Addictive entrepreneurs tend to invest their time, energy and moolah in the pursuit of success and undeterred by letdowns. They can also create employment for many, mentor other entrepreneurs and give back to the society in the form of social initiatives.

So go ahead and ask yourself if you are an addict. This simple question may make you feel uncomfortable. The human tendency is to automatically assume the question refers to consuming illegal narcotics or engaging in high-risk behaviors with potentially life-threatening consequences. In many instances, the word addiction has negative connotations. But along the business spectrum, being addicted to the thrill that comes from building success can unlock doors to nearly endless possibilities.

As a teenager and well into my twenties, I was obsessive. It's only when I heeded to society's whims that I tone it down and give up on the things I craved. But only to a point. It made my life sedentary and my creativity was stifled. My success started when I gave myself permission to fully own my obsession and use it to make positive change and to become an addict.

Entrepreneurship encourages, even rewards, addictive personalities. This single-mindedness can lead down pathways that reveal new strategies, services, products and lucrative financial opportunities. The progress at companies like Netflix, Apple, Amazon, and Tesla derives from company cultures that thrive when people are addicted to improvement and innovation.

Denying my obsession nearly killed me, foregoing what I really wanted to accomplish in life for a stable career in the US Army. I served nearly four and a half years in active duty and then about a year in the Ohio National Guard. I even went as far as becoming a cadet at the University of Cincinnati in their Reserve Officer Training Corps (R.O.T.C.). When I was leaving one of my cadet classes, the sergeant teaching the class told me, "You have something to tell me...don't you." I wasn't sure if he was asking or telling me. He went on to say, "You have no control over your life, and the chances are, this lifestyle is not the right one for you."

That was when I had to leave the military and I left the place fragile and broken, just as I had come in. Since I was no longer under the influence of a structured existence, my uncertainty about life and abilities were heightened. It was then I committed to using my addictive personality for success. Fifteen-plus years, five companies and tens of thousands of dollars later, I can attest that you must embrace your obsessions to embrace your inner entrepreneur.

Opening my arms and mind to embrace my relentless pursuit of entrepreneurial success did, in fact, produce positive results. Be forewarned, though acquiring a positive addiction wasn't any easier than creating a sustainable business. Along the way, I faced challenges such as securing startup capital and fostering support from my family and friends necessary to develop a viable business. But with discipline, I continue to attain goals by expecting the best while realizing the worst could happen before any new venture is successful.

I tried to work with practical methods to blend my passion with business. It's possible to have more than one area of intense interest in your life. However, if your intention is to create an addiction to business success, it's critical to focus on one passion at a time. This is how I built bridges from products to services and generated profits. Identifying my passion was easy. Focusing my efforts in one passion at a time was (and still is) a challenge. It helps when I examine the activities I enjoy. For example, if you love to braid your daughter's hair, and make it a point to do it regularly, think about how you could open your own hair salon. And if you're stumped by how to connect your passion with a business idea, ask others what they believe to be your best skills or abilities. Their answers might surprise you.

It's important to note that passion alone will not create business success. But it often is the starting point to design a well-structured business plan. After all, incorporating your deepest interests with your products or services is a pretty solid way to make sure you remain personally invested in your business. A few entrepreneurs roll the dice, gamble it all and laugh their way to success. Their stories become case studies for others to learn lessons. Even if their profits don't pay off, they take it all in stride and move on to the next opportunity with a brave heart and a smile on their face. However, there are others who keep moving ahead, but fail to recognize the tipping point at which entrepreneurship becomes too addictive to pursue.

Entrepreneurship addiction can possibly go very wrong really quick and in a hurry; at times becoming detrimental to our well-being and relationships. Here are a few ways you can develop a positive addiction to being an entrepreneur.

Step 1: Ask a similar series of questions every single day.

This simple task is essential to converting problems into profitable solutions. Pinpoint the questions that overlap your business and personal life and integrate them as a mantra to start every morning. Questions that probe your market's strengths and weaknesses can be excellent tools to apply to your business life. For personal matters, questions should be more focused on individual improvement. The right answers can help you become a more mindful partner, friend, or parent. Answering closely related questions over a series of time creates a consistent routine. It can reveal strategies that apply to entrepreneurial as well as personal achievements.

Step 2: Listen to your market.

Observe human behaviors and create specific goals you wish to align with a market. Take a moment and slow down. Listen to the needs and wants of your customers, family members, and friends with the intention of understanding them more fully. The gateway to all success begins with getting clarity on a problem, creating a plan and, taking action toward what you perceive is the best solution. Listening to the market can trigger the necessary connections between dreaming about success and growing addicted to work that has the potential to produce results.

Step 3: Fix Your Own Problems.

Attending high school in the 1990's, I was inundated with the exploration outside of myself to find causes to my most internal problems. At the time, a huge industry developed around the idea that our parents gave us either too little attention or too much. This was the era when the term dysfunctional family became omnipresent in our social lexicon. And once we realized that our family was dysfunctional, then we could reach into our inner child to begin to resolve our problems.

Back then, I thought that I was powerless, and I was predetermined to never get over it. I know now that this was not true and we should not place blame on our parents and factors outside our control. Stop blaming others and making excuses for your life.

Step 4: Know that you are in the Pilot's Seat.

When I began seeing myself as an entrepreneur, I was surrounded by what seemed to be the whole world telling me that I wasn't good enough. People told me my nontraditional experience was nothing special. You see, my peers consisted of urban planners, architects, Fortune 500 executives and the like. Me being a non-commissioned officer in the intelligence branch of the United States Army, working as a Korean linguist, did not equate.

Realize that you have control of your life, stop blaming others, and simply give yourself permission to become obsessed with the right things in life. Every great entrepreneur is an addict—and this isn't a bad thing at all.

Live Small But Dream Big

"Success is to be measured not so much by the position that one has reached in life as by the obstacles which he has overcome while trying to succeed." — Booker T. Washington

Covington is a city in Kenton County, Kentucky, placed right at the confluence of the Ohio and Licking Rivers. Cincinnati, Ohio lies to its north across the Ohio River and Newport, Kentucky, to its east across the Licking River. Part of the Cincinnati–Northern Kentucky metropolitan area, Covington has a population of about 40,500, with the population of the entire Greater Cincinnati population being just over 2 million, making Covington the fifth-most populous city in Kentucky.

Telling people that you were raised in a city like Covington, Kentucky, people from other parts of the United States are more prone to ask the number of cows that you had on your farm rather than where you went to college. Surprisingly, Covington is a jewel all unto itself. When I start to conjure words about Covington, many descriptions float to the tip of my tongue. If you are a visitor from out of town, you may only see Covington as a thoroughfare to get to Cincinnati from the airport (Cincinnati's airport is actually in Northern Kentucky) or simply, Cincinnati's southern sister city. During the time when the United States believed that slavery was a viable way of life, to African- Americans, Covington was a welcomed stop on en route north. But still, though in a southern state, Covington is a very urban city. So, growing up, space was a hot commodity.

And living in a small but mighty town like Covington, it's all in who you know. Does this sound familiar? As an entrepreneur, I don't have to tell you how important networking, forging partnerships, and just getting out there in front of your target audience is. But, if you're a natural introvert like I am, this can be a bit challenging, forcing yourself to step outside of your social comfort zone. But, here's the hard truth. To be successful in business, you must have confidence...and a lot of it!

Just look at the people behind some of the most successful businesses in the world and you'll notice that they are oozing with self-confidence. And, here's the good news… you don't have to be born with confidence. In fact, you can learn to be more comfortable and build your confidence over time. Just like the manner in which Covington was incorporated is nothing big. But those who incorporated the city had to think big.

In 1814, John Gano, Richard Gano, and Thomas Carneal purchased 150 acres on the west side of the Licking River at its confluence with the Ohio River, referred to as "The Point," from Thomas Kennedy for $50,000. The men named their new riverfront enterprise the Covington Company, in honor of their friend, Gen. Leonard Covington, an officer in the military who trained troops in the area and was killed in the War of 1812. The investors created a space for their new city only five blocks wide by five blocks deep. The streets lined up perfectly with the streets of Cincinnati across the Ohio River, symbolically tying the future of the fledgling city to its larger northern neighbor. The first five streets, running north to south, were named for Kentucky's first five governors: Shelby, Garrard, Greenup, Scott, and Madison.

PRESENTING, *MYSTERY BEHIND THE MURDER*, A LUNCH & LEARN SESSION ABOUT THE STORY OF MARGARET GARNER AND HER STORY OF SLAVERY, MURDER AND THE LAW.

Just like Covington's founders were, don't be afraid of change. Awareness is part of the process, but action is what gets you results. Once you realize that it's only your confidence that's holding you back, you need to be committed to wanting to change this. Otherwise, recognizing a problem without being willing to fix it, is just a waste of your time.

But how can we apply this to our time that we have throughout the day?

Have a clear plan. Just like other goals, confidence improvement is best attacked with a good and clear plan. You need to be focused and dedicated to achieving your goal. But, you must first have one. And, if you really want to accelerate your growth, challenge yourself to go big, or go home. Write your plan down to make it easier for you to monitor your progress. Don't be afraid to try something radically different, like giving a keynote speech or registering to present at an upcoming business conference. Not only will this force you to actively work on your confidence, but it will be a great way for you to see how much you have improved (or what additional work you may need to do).

Take care of yourself. When you make your health (including your mental health) a priority, you will begin to feel good. And when you feel good, you start to see your value and appreciate yourself more. You cannot grow your business or reach the level of success you deserve, if you are not well or don't have the energy to get up and go for your goals.

Create time saving techniques. Every entrepreneur knows how quickly time gets gobbled up. Before you know it, the day is over, and you still have about a dozen things that you need to accomplish. This is a common theme among all who pursue the excitement and rewards of any entrepreneurial endeavor, large or small. While the adage, "Work smarter, not harder," simply isn't as easy as it sounds, entrepreneurs of all industries can increase efficiency by tweaking their routine to squeeze more time out of the day. One thing that you should ask yourself is if you deem yourself efficient as an entrepreneur. If you really want to save time and crush your goals, first make the structure of your business your first priority.

Sure, the very nature of being an entrepreneur means bucking the system and doing your own thing. However, it is essential to keep structure at your foundation to save time. By making structure a priority, you will find those daily tasks and weekly projects being checked off in a very timely manner. Structure allows you to focus more on the future, rather than staying focused on just one thing. Placing importance on being more structured will also rub off on your team. Your flair for structure, time management, and efficiency will make those you work with find organizational structure beneficial. Make it contagious among your team.

Always learn and improve. One way to boost your self-confidence is by showing yourself that you can effectively learn from your mistakes and improve your work. When you are confident in your ability to make your mistakes work for you, you become willing to try new things and go for your goals. In case you fail, you know you can easily bounce back. And, it is 100% okay to be a work in progress – just stay focused on learning and improving.

Do things that scare you. Fear and low confidence go hand in hand to form a vicious cycle. When you are afraid of so many things, your confidence suffers, which makes you afraid of change or making big decisions. Being an entrepreneur is not for the faint of heart. You will make mistakes. You will have to take risks. You will have to give up control. This is where getting out there and networking with other business owners can be a great resource, so you can get mentoring and advice to help guide you on your entrepreneurial journey. Remember, you will lose out on every opportunity that you don't take.

Take "switching costs" out of your daily time budget. The cost of time it takes you to switch from one task to another, also known as multitasking, actually wastes time. Schedule a task, focus on it completely, and then move on to the next one.

Cut toxic people out of your life. Sometimes, your lack of confidence comes from what other people are telling you. Sadly, there are really people out there who just like putting others down. They do this out of insecurity, habit, and plenty of other reasons. Regardless of their reasons for hurting other people's feelings, you have every right to shut them out when they are not feeding you positivity and encouragement.

Don't forget to celebrate your achievements. Poor self-confidence is often partnered with disregarding your success. You berate yourself for your errors, but completely ignore the things you do well. Learn to pat yourself on the back for every achievement, big or small. Acknowledging your achievements is not a bad thing. In fact, it gives you the motivation to want to do even more and reach your lofty goals.

Here's the bottom-line…

If you want to make it as an entrepreneur, you will need to be confident in your decisions and confident in yourself. Even the best business idea, most advanced Internet marketing tools, or top-notch employees can't help you if you don't invest the time in building your own self-confidence. Remember, it's a marathon, not a sprint, so make a goal to improve and work toward it – no matter what!

Time To Shit Or Get Off The Pot

"If you fail to plan, you are planning to fail." -Benjamin Franklin

In 2016, I, like most of America that year, experienced a sort of temporal acceleration. It was nothing short of vertigo-inducing. In April, I found myself unemployed, contemplating a huge shift of my living situation and, basically, feeling as though I had no place in this world. This, of course, was on top of how President Donald Trump shocked the world (and I think himself as well) by tricking America into letting him become president. And this is when I envisioned how to reinvent my business model.

We all constantly have great business ideas, but sometimes they fail because we just don't know how to turn those daydreams into reality. And most of the time it's probably because you don't have the experience to know what to do next. Even when you think that you have an original idea, no business idea is totally unique. There will always be businesses out there that are like yours. So, don't sweat it if there are companies doing what you do. What it tells you is that there's a market for what you do. What you do have to think about is who your competition will be, what exactly they are providing and what you will do differently or better than they do.

To be sure, the things which I experienced in life don't compare to the most truly interesting moments that many in this world have experienced, but like not knowing what to do, the things that I went through, rocked my core and had me contemplating a number of things which I never thought of before, like kicking this entrepreneur thing in the ass. Just in 2018, close to 550,000 people, according to the Kauffman startup index, become entrepreneurs each month... so why can't you be one of them?

As you know, the actual formula for success eludes us, but there are steps which can be taken to get you closer to it.

First, take a look at what you are already doing.

If this entrepreneurial thing is as foreign to you as a night in Bangkok, its best to find your start by doing what you are already doing. Do you like styling your girlfriends hair? Be the person who finds a quick and easy style that you can easily reproduce and begin your own home business.

Bam. Now you're in business.

To be clearer, you are your own best solution to your own problems. Stray away from looking to fix other people's problems. Execute your ideas and disrupt the paradigm of your own life. Even if it means making the most simplistic of gadgets with toilet paper rolls and clothes pins. Just know that having something tangible, something that you can feel and touch, makes a world of difference. But don't stop there, brag about it, show it off, get buy-in from your friends and followers on social media and then keep on truckin' by gathering feedback, implementing adjustments, and then repeat.

Now before you go and lock yourself in your basement, you better be in it for the long haul. This process can get long and repetitive real quick and in a hurry. That is why the problem that you are destined to solve needs to be one that haunts your soul. I cannot emphasize this enough.

What worked for me? I connected with like-minded people and gave back to my community. All of you reading this are in the early stages of breaking into entrepreneur-realism, a stage where you are going to need things from other people. By surrounding yourself with those who share your mindset for entrepreneurship, outside of keeping you motivated, they can scratch your back and you can scratch theirs. When you network, you should not only focus on what you want out of it, but also figure out what you are able to give back. What are your skills? Asking myself that very same question, I tend to seek out mentorship in creative and inspirational design esthetic in exchange for my expertise in business and fund development. As with any good relationship, this new connection becomes meaningful when it exemplifies itself into a two-way street.

THE TWO MOST INFLUENTIAL PEOPLE IN MY LIFE, MY MOTHER KATHERINE (LEFT) AND MY GRANDMOTHER LILLIAN (RIGHT).

Next, you need to figure out how to concentrate on the "why" and "who" of your new business idea. You may think you've thought up an awesome idea, but it is imperative that you know the real reasons behind why it's a good solution, or your business won't be successful. To stand out from the competition, you will need to know what sets you apart. Start doing research on the companies that could become your competition. Look at how much they charge, who their target audience is, and how they market, to name just a few research points. There's no need to reinvent the wheel but do look at what these companies are lacking in and how you can improve upon those areas in your business, so that you capture their customers.

After you've taken a deep dive into why your business is needed in the first place, determine who will be the target audience of your business. Think about the demographics of your target audience, what's important to these people and how you will reach them. A business isn't a business without customers, after all.

Next, use your immediate and potential competition to study potential customers. Locate them and start engaging them to see if your product or service is something they would use. Find out how much they would pay for it and ask what comparable product or business they're using now to solve the problem. You can also begin to nail down the answers to the following:

Will you be offering a product or a service?

How much will it cost?

How will you be marketing your business?

You need to know your new business concept inside and out before you launch and getting input from potential customers could help. Also, if you haven't named your business yet, now's the time to do it. Do some brainstorming and come up with a name that no one else has already taken.

And after you've worked out all the details of your future business, the next step is to figure out how to turn your dream into a reality. Obviously starting a business could cost quite a bit of money, so that's one of the major "how" factors you need to consider. Decide if you'll talk to investors, take out a loan, or maybe even start a crowdsource campaign. Determine everything you'll need to get your business up and running. For instance, if you're offering a product, how will you build it and how much money will it cost to build? This last step is one of the most important in order to take your business from out of your head and into the real world.

This all lends itself to investing in the time to create a succinct business plan. A business plan is a very important strategic tool for entrepreneurs. A good business plan not only helps entrepreneurs to focus on the specific steps necessary for them to make business ideas succeed, but it also helps them to achieve both their short-term and long-term objectives. While a business plan is absolutely essential in entrepreneurship, not every entrepreneur sees the need for it. Many are reluctant to have their plan written down. In fact, there are numerous articles online claiming that the business plan is dead or irrelevant. Of course, not everyone agrees with that.

A large number of business funding experts agree that having a good business idea is not enough. Even excellent business ideas can be totally useless if you cannot formulate, execute, and implement a strategic plan to make your business idea work.

If you're looking to raise funds from institutional investors and lenders, keep in mind that having a good business plan is extremely valuable. You should aim to have a well-documented business plan that speaks for itself. It needs to be clear and easy to read and understand. Creating a business plan involves a lot of thought. You need to consider what you want to do and use that as a starting point. It doesn't need to be complicated. At its core, your plan should identify where you are now, where you want your business to go, and how you will get there.

One thing that I've discovered, since I have surpassed the big 4-0, my tolerance for mediocrity is disappearing, and I love bringing this mindset over onto my entrepreneurial space. It's literally like someone flipped a switch and I became a black male version of Faye Dunaway's portrayal of Joan Crawford in the film Mommy Dearest. Ask yourself the following; what value are you providing to the one who buys your product, idea, or service? Remember, they are the people who are actually using and benefiting from your hard work. How will they extract value and what process will you use to earn money? Once you have these questions nailed down, you just might be on your way to something special...something unique.

In September 1990, I was a ninth grader living with my mother, and my two younger brothers, and my stepfather. The city was in the midst of the War on Drugs, with the battlefield manifesting itself in Covington's black, low-income neighborhoods. We lived in the Westside neighborhood of Covington, which was a part of the city that had its pockets of crime but was mostly a solid mix of blue-collar and poverty-stricken families. I was attending Covington Latin High School, a college preparatory school that had a solid reputation for success and I was learning Latin and advanced algebra at the age of 12, the age I was admitted into the high school as a freshman.

I was also the only black student in the entire high school and nothing I had experienced before then prepared me for this type of culture shock. The difference between me and my new classmates was that nearly all of them had never attended class with a black person. In contrast, all of my teachers had been white and, surprisingly, my prior Catholic school education afforded me a very mixed-race education. At that age, white people were just there. White people in black spaces were common. For example, the television show "In Living Color" made Jim Carrey into a star. But now, I was a black child in a white space, too young and naive to realize how much of a big deal this was. But it soon dawned on me the gravity of the situation. Like when I joined the school's basketball team. Now, truth be told, there hasn't ever been a part of me that was inherently athletic. I've always had to work hard at it. And at the time, I was definitely one of the worst players on the team. But weird enough, I was one of the high scorers on our team that year. Hard work? Maybe. Or could it be the fact that the ball was always thrown my way with the assumption that I was a good basketball player and I would make the shot.

During my time at Covington Latin, I was very lonely at first, feeling like a specimen in a lab. I didn't like the attention. In fact, I hated the attention. I had to begin performing self-care before it was a thing. I would use the solitude found in books as my sanctuary. I buried my head in books and artwork. I would sit outside and draw. Or sit in my room and read. Also, going into this situation, I knew that I would have to work twice as hard to be considered just as good in this school. And that I was being watched closely, not only by those inside the school, but also by those in the black community, the one who really wanted me to succeed so I tried to become the model minority.

Well, if you know me, that didn't work.

Many black people will never be comfortable in an all-white space. I can thrive in one. I had to for several years. Now, I am somewhat comfortable with all-white spaces. This skill has proven to be helpful in many situations, such as during my military career when I was one of a half dozen black soldiers in an army company that totaled several hundred. But even if I'm the only black person in the room, I'll never love being the only black person in the room, but I have grown to push it to the back of my mind.

Throughout my life, mostly because of the aforementioned, I have been told that I talk funny. I've heard in more times than times then I can count. I began hearing this during my first year in high school right up until a recent trip to San Francisco. It could be because of the mixture of my southern and Midwestern background, and my attempt to get rid of it as I've grown older. It probably has something to do with me wanting to say things they you learn in school. Put them all together and you get me talking in a funny way.

So, go ahead, re-watch the 1981 classic film *Mommy Dearest* where the abusive and traumatic adoptive upbringing at the hands of her mother, a screen queen is depicted and talk funny.

I talk funny, because I think funny. Which has helped me succeed as an entrepreneur.